the essence of
Buddhism

the essence of
Buddhism

How to bring spiritual meaning into every day

Carole M. Cusack

RAINCOAST BOOKS

Vancouver

Contents

Introduction

Buddhism is one of the world's great religions. Founded more than two and a half thousand years ago in India, it has certain ideas in common with the other great Indian religions, *Hinduism*[1] and *Jainism*. Today it continues to grow in strength, with followers drawn primarily from Asia, Europe, the Americas and Australia. It is based on the teachings of **Siddhartha Gautama**,[2] known as the *Buddha* ('Enlightened One'), who lived in the sixth century BC in what is now northern India and Nepal.

The footprints of Buddha.

Unique among religions

Buddhism contains a diversity of practices and a flexibility of beliefs which make it unique among religions:

- Rather than having a god or the divine realm as its focal point, it concentrates on the dilemmas of the human condition.
- The Buddha, its originator, understood what it was like to possess material comforts, to live with a loving family and to have dear friends, and yet to feel unsatisfied and to yearn to know the meaning of human existence.
- The teachings the Buddha developed as a result of his enlightenment experience are a practical, step-by-step guide to release from the cravings that plague human life.
- The Buddha's teachings are also a guide to achieving both serenity and the ability to 'see things as they really are.'

1. All terms in *italics* appear in the Glossary.
   Note that italics are used only the first time the term appears in this book.
2. All names in **bold** appear in the List of Names.
   Note that bold is used only the first time the name appears in this book.

Buddhism groups

Buddhism's reliance on very basic doctrine, as well as its flexibility with religious practices, means that there are in fact many 'Buddhisms,' with regional variations. Traditionally, there have been three groups.

Buddhism group	Meaning	Where found
Theravada	'tradition of the elders'	Laos, Sri Lanka, Thailand
Mahayana	'great vehicle'	China, Japan, Vietnam
Vajrayana	'diamond vehicle'	Mongolia, Nepal, Tibet

The great number of Western converts throughout the twentieth century has resulted in a new, fourth group, the Western Buddhists. This group makes use of elements from all the groups, and has developed some of its own distinctive practices.

For most Western Buddhists the essence of Buddhism rests in the life story of the Buddha, and the example he set in achieving enlightenment and insisting that it is achievable by all. The Buddha rejected the more limiting elements of the Hindu faith in which he had been brought up in favor of a powerful self-help philosophy.

Using the Buddha's teachings to arrive at a right understanding of life, everyone can take control of their spiritual destiny, meditate, and achieve enlightenment.

The principle that people should act for themselves, rather than succumbing to the actions of an all-powerful god, remains one of Buddhism's most attractive features.

Beginnings of Buddhism

Who was Buddha?

Born to wealth and power, young Siddhartha Gautama was a prince of the north Indian Shakya clan in the sixth century BC. His father **Shuddodhana** provided him with every luxury, and was strangely restrictive at the same time. Until the age of twenty-nine Siddhartha had never been outside the confines of his father's vast palace, where only beauty, health, happiness and love were to be found. His happiness was complete when his loving wife **Yasodhara** gave birth to a son, **Rahula**. But was it? Siddhartha was troubled, as many people today are, by the question: 'What is the meaning of life?'

Siddhartha was as yet unaware that a great destiny awaited him. His father's restrictiveness was actually the result of a prophecy made at Siddhartha's birth. A sage had told the father that if his princely son ever saw an old person, a sick person, or a corpse, he would abandon his life of pleasure and become a beggar monk, seeking enlightenment.

Siddhartha's curiosity eventually took him beyond the confines of the palace, and the prophecy came to pass: he left his wife and child as they slept, and with a heavy heart began to seek enlightenment. His father grieved, but could not stop his son from fulfilling his spiritual destiny. This departure was a radical step. Hindu tradition decreed that if you were born a warrior, that was the life path you should follow. Retirement for the purpose of piety and devotion was permissible in old age, but Siddhartha was in his prime and had duties and responsibilities. Yet he could not resist the call to achieve enlightenment.

From Hinduism to Buddhism

Siddhartha was born a Hindu, of the caste of the warriors, and the idea of enlightenment was current in this faith.

In his views, the Buddha retained the Hindu belief in the cycle of birth and rebirth, but insisted that enlightenment, here called *nirvana* (meaning 'cooled' or 'quenched'), could be achieved by people of all *castes*, and by women as well as men.

Vitarka-mudra: symbol of doctrine and reasoning.

Reincarnation and karma

- The Hindu belief in reincarnation is the belief that the soul or spiritual part of a person does not die when the body dies, but moves on to inhabit another body, and to have another life.

- It is believed by Hindus that enlightenment (usually called *moksha*, 'liberation') could only be achieved after many reincarnations, and after finally being reborn with the high status of a male *Brahmin* (priest).

- The quality of this next life depends on the *karma* that the person acquired in his or her previous life.

- Karma means 'action.' All intentional actions, whether physical, verbal or mental, are karma. An action is seen as good or bad depending on the intention that motivates it. Good, or virtuous, actions are the main cause of rebirth in the higher realms. Bad, or non-virtuous, actions are the main cause of rebirth in the lower realms.

Founding a movement

It is not clear that Siddhartha intended to found a movement called 'Buddhism.' His quest, when he set out into the world, was for personal enlightenment. Having become enlightened, he was obligated to assist others in their quest for nirvana. He gently discouraged people from becoming his disciples. His charismatic personality and authoritative teaching attracted followers, however, and during his preaching years he acquired five hundred disciples. He died after after forty-five years of preaching work, on the way to a small town called Kusinara, near the Nepalese border. At the hour of his death he told his followers:

> *And now, my monks, I take my leave of you; all the elements of being are transitory; work out your own salvation with diligence.*

Siddhartha's kinsman **Ananda** took over as the leader of the community, but the Buddha's last words suggested that anyone could achieve enlightenment by their own efforts, even outside the community. Buddha had unusual psychological gifts, and was aware of the difficulties which people faced. Often it was not enough to have heard his preaching and have accepted his diagnosis of what was wrong in human life: many people needed to be helped along the way.

Buddha reclining in the state of parinirvana — the trance of complete liberation from which one cannot return from earthly life.

The preaching Buddha.

The foundation of Buddhism is best viewed as the result of Buddha's followers desiring to be organized into a movement where they could pursue common goals.

The paramount virtue in Buddha's ethical system was compassion (see pages 22–23), and this meant that the formation of a community was inevitable. The independent and unorganized life of the forest sages could not be pursued by large numbers of people. There were practical advantages to coming together as a group. It was recognized that each person's search for enlightenment was an individual matter, but the support and concern of the group could lift the spirits and prevent disciples falling away through becoming discouraged. Therefore, the Buddha, who did not desire followers and did not wish to set himself up as anything other than a man who had become enlightened, accepted the responsibility of leading a monastic and lay community.

The Path to Enlightenment

Torment in the forest

Starting out on the journey to enlightenment, Siddhartha took the traditional Hindu path. He retired to the forest, where he practiced various types of yoga.

Siddhartha studied with two venerable spiritual teachers, **Alara Kalama** and **Uddaka Ramaputta**. He also listened to the philosophical arguments of five *bhikkus* (monks) whose acquaintance he had made. He subjected his body to terrible torments of asceticism. He strove to control his body by restraining his breath and controlling his heartbeat. He sat among thorns and endured other types of pain. It is recorded that he lived for seven years on a single bowl of rice, and that when he pressed his hand to his stomach he could feel his spine.

Siddhartha lived at the time of the forest ascetics. These men were often of the warrior caste, like Siddhartha, and dissatisfied with the official religious answers.

The thoughts of the forest ascetics are preserved in the *Upanishads*. 'Upa' means 'near,' 'ni' means 'down,' and 'shad' means 'to sit.' An upanishad is a teaching given to a pupil by a *rishi* ('master'), when the pupil sits at the feet of the master.

The forest masters sought to be freed from the reincarnation cycle of birth, death and rebirth through the practice of yoga and meditation. Many of their teachings were about the need to reject the things of the world. The Katha Upanishad teaches that the pleasure of worldly things is not actually enjoyable because it is undermined by the threat of old age, disease and death. Worldly things are therefore illusions, and should be thoroughly rejected in order to achieve liberation.

Dharmachakra: Veneration of Buddha turning the 'Wheel of Law'.

Yet, deep down, Siddhartha was not convinced that such physical hardship could result in enlightenment. Enlightenment, to him, meant complete freedom from the anxieties of life, a state where there are no further reincarnations and the *atman* (soul) is at peace. If he was deliberately starving himself and trying to control his body, this meant he was still caught up in the anxieties of life. At this time he said:

> How can enlightenment be reached by a man who is not
> calm and at ease, who is so exhausted by hunger and thirst that
> his mind is unbalanced?

Though he had pursued a path of physical self-denial for several years, he was still unenlightened.

Toward moderation

So Siddhartha accepted a bowl of rice in milk from a compassionate young village girl, **Sujata** (sometimes called **Nandabala**), and began to regain his health. The five bhikkus were disgusted that he could indulge himself in this way and left him at once. But Siddhartha was convinced of the rightness of his decision. His life so far had consisted of complete luxury, followed by complete deprivation. It was time to try moderation. He was thirty-five years old, and determined to attain nirvana.

Sitting under the Bodhi tree

Siddhartha sat in the lotus position under a fig tree in a place called *Bodh-gaya*. This tree has become known to Buddhists as the *Bodhi* ('knowledge') tree. Cuttings have been taken to monasteries all over Asia, and some are flourishing still.

Seated under the fig tree, Siddhartha resolved to become enlightened. He vowed:

Never from this seat will I stir,
until I have attained the supreme
and absolute wisdom.

He was seen by the god **Mara**, variously described as the god of Love or Desire, or as a demon of illusion. Mara wanted to prevent Siddhartha from becoming enlightened. He summoned his three sons, Flurry, Gaiety and Sullen Pride, and then his three daughters, Discontent, Delight and Thirst.

The Bodhi tree – the knowledge tree under which Siddhartha sat awaiting enlightenment.

- ☉ **In the first watch** of the night, Siddhartha reviewed all of his previous lives and incarnations, understanding completely the cycle of rebirth and the suffering that prolongs it. These previous lives are recorded in the *Mahavastu* ('Great Event'), a biography of the Buddha. They include the life of **Mahasattva**, a prince who sacrificed himself to feed a tigress that was dying of hunger; and **Kshantivardin** ('preacher of patience'), a forest ascetic. Because one who is to become a buddha must be compassionate above all things, the stories about Buddha's past lives generally emphasize the virtue of compassion.

- ☉ **In the second watch** of the night, Siddhartha's sight became true as he achieved the Heavenly Eye. This meant that he could see through all of the illusions of the world.

- ☉ **In the third watch**, he comprehended the true nature of existence.

- ☉ **And in the fourth watch** he attained enlightenment.

They launched themselves at Siddhartha, attempting to break his resolve.

Siddhartha's calmness and firmness defeated them. He pointed to the earth, asking that it be witness to his worthiness of achieving the state of a buddha (enlightened being). Mara and his daughters were routed by Siddhartha's spiritual excellence. They watched with fury as he left the human state behind, entering into the final stage before achieving buddhahood.

Bhumisparsha-mudra: symbol of witness to enlightenment.

Buddha pointing to the earth, asking that it be witness to his worthiness of achieving the state of a buddha.

An enlightened being

After the defeat of Mara, Siddhartha became a *bodhisattva* – 'one who is going to become a buddha.' He entered a meditative trance, and as he sat through the night he became enlightened.

The poet **Ashvaghosha** (first century AD), author of the *Buddhacarita* ('Acts of the Buddha'), says that the whole of creation rejoiced at Siddhartha's enlightenment. Only Mara felt bitter, and diminished by his defeat. The weather was beautiful, and all realms, from the lowest hell to the highest heaven, yearned toward the *dharma* ('law'). Siddhartha, now the Buddha (enlightened one), sat for seven days in a state of bliss. He described his transformation thus:

In me emancipated arose the knowledge of my emancipation.
I realized that rebirth is destroyed, the religious life has been led,
done is what was to be done, there is nought [for me] beyond this
world ... Ignorance was dispelled, knowledge arose. Darkness was
dispelled, light arose.

When he had assimilated this state, he considered how, and to whom, he should communicate his knowledge. As his old masters Alara Kalama and Uddaka Ramaputta had died, he resolved to teach the five bhikkus. He traveled to Sarnath. Here he was reunited with the five bhikkus, and his active preaching life began. It was to last forty-five years.

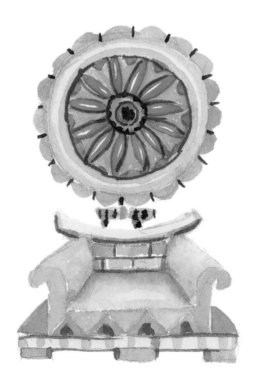

A monastic community

The first Buddhist monks were the five bhikkus who were present at the Buddha's First Sermon in Sarnath. Through their ordination, Buddha inaugurated the *sangha* – the Buddhist monastic community. Lay Buddhists also converted, but the sangha enjoys the special status of a 'community dedicated to enlightenment.'

Legend says that Buddha then traveled to Kapilavastu to preach the dharma (law) to his father Shuddodhana, who heard it with joy. During this visit he saw his wife Yasodhara, and received his son Rahula into the sangha. He then went to the heavens to preach to his mother **Maya** and the gods. He organized the sangha, and set out the basic rules for the monastic life, which involved adherence to the *Ten Precepts* (see page 25).

The life of the monks was one of wandering throughout India in the fine season, preaching and begging, and taking retreats during the summer monsoon season. In the Buddha's lifetime these retreats were often conducted in caves in northern India, but disciples later gave the Buddhists land and buildings.

When the number of monks in the sangha reached sixty, Buddha sent them out as missionaries, authorizing his monks to ordain other monks. A chain of monasteries and places of retreat was formed all over the country.

Buddhist spirituality

Some of the earliest insights into Buddhist spirituality were produced by monks and bhikkuni (nuns) in their retreats during the rainy season. They composed poems, called therigatha ('songs of the elders'), which were often very personal. In early times they were written on the walls of the caves into which the sangha retreated. Here is an example:

Dhyana-mudra: symbol of meditation.

In the woodland thickets beyond Ambataka park
His craving pulled up by the root, lucky Bhaddiyya lives
In meditation. Though some like the music of drums
Or the cymbals and mandolins, my delight as I sit
By a tree is the sound of the Buddha's message. And if
The Buddha would grant me a wish and the wish were mine,
I would choose that the whole world might constantly
Be alert to the transience of all physical things.

Buddha's disciples

Buddha's chief disciples from early on were **Sariputta** and **Moggallana**, and these were later joined by Ananda, Buddha's relative and most beloved disciple. **Devadatta**, another cousin, played the role of the 'Buddhist Judas' – he caused a split in the sangha through his jealousy of Ananda. His wickedness resulted in attacks on the life of Buddha. A frenzied elephant was set upon him, and on another occasion a huge rock was rolled at him from a hilltop. Buddha escaped unharmed, and eventually the community lost patience with Devadatta and he departed.

Another family member, Buddha's aunt and foster-mother **Mahaprajapati** (her name means 'great perfection of wisdom'), shaved her head and appeared before Buddha in the saffron robes of a monk, requesting to be ordained as a bhikkuni.

Buddha was initially doubtful about the value of establishing an order of nuns. He feared that their admission would devalue the reputation of Buddhism and create administrative difficulties with the regulation of relations between the sexes.

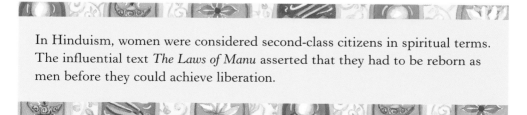

In Hinduism, women were considered second-class citizens in spiritual terms. The influential text *The Laws of Manu* asserted that they had to be reborn as men before they could achieve liberation.

But Ananda argued for the admission of women, and eventually Buddha was persuaded. He accepted Mahaprajapati, and founded the order of Buddhist nuns.

Women flocked to hear the Buddha's teachings and to seek enlightenment. Lay people in general were impressed by Buddha's rejection of the Hindu caste system. He insisted that all who sought enlightenment truly, whether priest, lord or peasant, could achieve it. The only requirement was a sincere devotion to the dharma, and a committed pursuit of the *Noble Eightfold Path*, a set of principles leading to the cessation of suffering (see pages 32–34).

Early Buddhism grew slowly as a movement, and for the first few centuries was primarily a monastic movement. Nevertheless, the small lay community supported the monks and nuns, who begged for their food. Lay Buddhists placed their faith in the 'Three Jewels' – the Buddha himself, the dharma (eternal law and truth, revealed in the Buddha's teachings) and the sangha.

Buddha's strenuous rejection of metaphysics and theology also endeared him to the people. In a conversation with a monk, Buddha said that metaphysical queries were like a person who had been wounded by an arrow and now desired to know all the details of the wounding. In contrast, a surgeon would concentrate on removing the arrow and healing the suffering person.

There is also an early story of Kisagotomi, a girl whose child had died. She asked Buddha to restore the child to life, and he said he would do so if she could get some herbs from a household where death had never struck. Kisagotomi made inquiries, but discovered that no one was free from death. She was then able to accept her baby's death.

Death of the Buddha

When he was about eighty, after forty-five years of preaching work, the Buddha prepared to die. The sangha was in a small town near the Nepalese border when he announced his imminent decease to Ananda. The details are recorded in a short text called *The Book of the Great Decease*. The Buddha said:

I am old now, Ananda, and full of years; my journey nears its end,
and I have reached my sum of days for I am nearly eighty years old.
So, Ananda, you must be your own lamps, be your own refuges.

Ananda wept, but Buddha, his death hastened by food poisoning, passed into the state called *parinirvana*. This is the trance of complete liberation, from which one cannot return to earthly life. These were his final words:

All the elements of being are transitory; work on
your own salvation with diligence.

Western scholars usually date the Buddha's death at 483 BC. The sangha cremated the sage's body, and collected his bones in reliquary jars, dividing them into eight parts. The bones were distributed around India, buried in structures called *stupas*. Ananda, assisted by another monk, **Upali**, had been left in charge of the community. Five hundred monks assembled for the first Buddhist council in Rajagaha, for the purpose of collecting the remembered teachings of the Buddha and planning for the future.

Above: Vara-mudra: symbol of compassion.
Right: Bodhidharma meditating in a cave.

Basic Principles of Buddhism

Suffering and compassion

Buddha had the gift of understanding humans' psychological make-up. This led him to assert that humans find life is filled with *dukkha* (the Sanskrit word for 'suffering'). Many who read of this assertion were reluctant to accept the grim diagnosis of the meaning of life, but became more reconciled once they realized that 'dukkha' could also mean 'unsatisfactoriness.'

As the Buddha perceived, even the most pleasant sensations in our lives can be unsatisfactory: they end too quickly, and they cause us to become addicts, yearning for more. Then we swing the full pendulum between overindulgence and self-discipline, and fail to achieve a balance.

Buddha saw that the most important thing, if people were to attain serenity, was to cut off the feelings of unsatisfactoriness at the source. He understood that it is a human tendency to crave the things we don't have, and to crave the prolongation of those we do. It is not sufficient to engage occasionally in physical or mental discipline in order to purify ourselves. Nor is it enough for us merely to seek pleasure in indulgence. He realized that a path had to be charted that would make it possible for people to become detached from craving. Then it would not be necessary either to overindulge or to deny oneself.

As Buddha saw it, being freed from the twin constraints of unsatisfactoriness and craving does not necessarily make us excessively 'religious' or 'spiritual.' We merely acquire the ability to see things as they really are; we achieve a state of serenity that is built on a foundation of true freedom.

In the Buddhist view, this freedom can be achieved by voluntarily undertaking to follow the Noble Eightfold Path (see pages 32–34) and to observe the Ten Precepts (see page 25). The final result will be a happiness few can imagine. This is explained at the beginning of the famous Buddhist scripture, the *Dhammapada*:

> *If a man speaks or acts with a pure thought,*
> *happiness follows him, like a shadow that never leaves him.*
> *'He abused me, he beat me, he defeated me, he robbed me' –*
> *in those who harbour such thoughts, hatred will never cease;*
> *in those who do not harbour such thoughts,*
> *hatred will cease. For hatred does not cease by hatred at any*
> *time; hatred ceases by love – this is an old rule.*

The characteristic sign that a person has achieved this state is a display of compassion – the supreme Buddhist virtue – toward all creatures. Compassion is active, it is humanitarian, and it connects with all beings in a way that avoids dangerous or injurious attachments. Compassion does not seek to avoid difficult situations, nor does it desire that people be 'let off' lightly. It involves the firm and unflinching acceptance of situations as they truly are, and seeks the solution to problems with realism and determination.

Bhaisajya-guru: the Buddha as the Great Doctor for the Ills of the World.

Detachment and engagement

Buddhism is often portrayed by its detractors as an unworldly and unrealistic belief system. This generally occurs because the Buddhist notion of detachment has been misunderstood.

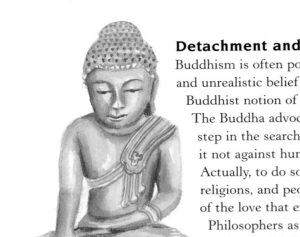

The Buddha advocated the cessation of cravings as a necessary step in the search for enlightenment. But how can this be? Is it not against human nature to seek love without attachment? Actually, to do so is a commandment found in many world religions, and people have always recognized the high virtue of the love that expects no reciprocal emotion or reward.

Philosophers as diverse as Socrates (5th century BC) and Simone Weill (20th century AD) have suggested that selflessness is the foundation of the ethical life. This is not to suggest that it is an easy thing to achieve. However, the very difficulty involved has been enough to convince many people of the worthiness of the enterprise.

A Burmese seated Buddha.

The Buddhist is not commanded to separate himself or herself from the world, or from the needs of other people. On the contrary, the Buddhist masters his or her desires in order to engage more purely with the world. Buddhism, like Hinduism, does not have a notion of 'sin,' because, in the Buddha's understanding, there is no 'sin' — there are only false views and ignorance. Evil does not stem from a negative principle or a devil, but from ignorance. Once false views are eradicated, a person will cause no more evil. Detachment and the absence of desire are essential for the cessation of evil.

The Ten Precepts

The ethical conduct of Buddhist monks and nuns is regulated by the Ten Precepts:

1. Refrain from destroying life.
2. Do not take what is not given.
3. Abstain from unchastity.
4. Do not lie or deceive.
5. Abstain from intoxicants.
6. Eat moderately and before midday.
7. Do not watch dancing, singing or theatrical spectacles.
8. Do not wear garlands, perfumes, cosmetics or ornaments.
9. Do not sleep in high or wide beds.
10. Do not accept gold or silver.

The revolutionary nature of the Ten Precepts lies in the way they illustrate the *Middle Way*, the path of moderation advocated by the Buddha. Overindulgence in pleasures is warned against, but ascetic self-denial is not advocated.

The first precept concerns the fundamental Buddhist principle of *ahimsa*, doing no harm, and is the most important of the ten. Lay followers of Buddhism are obliged to live by the first five of these Ten Precepts. The extra duties and commitments of the monks and nuns are an inspiration for the lay Buddhist. If Buddhism has a 'creed,' it is the declaration of reliance upon the 'Three Jewels':

⊚ I take refuge in the Buddha;
⊚ I take refuge in the dharma (teachings);
⊚ I take refuge in the sangha (monastic order).

The Buddhist understanding of the self

⊚ In Hinduism, there is a belief in an individual soul (atman) which is reunited with the world-soul (*Brahman*) when enlightenment is reached. One of the most challenging doctrines of the Buddha is the doctrine of *anatta*, often translated as 'no self' or 'no soul'– a negation of the existence of the world-soul. This was a radical departure from his Hindu upbringing.

⊚ Buddha believed that there was little value in spending precious mental energy on speculative subjects such as the gods or the nature of the divine. Hence his rejection of the world-soul.

⊚ Buddha also considered the question of the individual soul. It is important to realize that his use of the term 'soul' incorporates aspects of what we would consider to be the ego or the will, and is far more psychological than theological. He rejected the individual soul too.

⊚ Buddha's rejection of the individual human ego follows naturally from his doctrines of the necessity of detachment and the value of selfless interaction with others. If people assign value to themselves, whether to their bodies, minds, or spiritual parts ('souls'), they will continue to be attached to themselves and to be distracted from the goal of enlightenment.

Abhaya-mudra:
symbol of protection.

⊚ In Buddhism, true knowledge of our own reality consists in acknowledging that one is impermanent and ultimately insignificant, although this may not seem the case on occasion.

Enlightenment

Despite the central importance of nirvana (enlightenment) to the meaning of life, Buddha did not like talking about it. He generally defined it negatively, which also makes it elusive to grasp. One famous definition is that nirvana is:

> *The extinction of desire, the extinction of hatred,*
> *the extinction of illusion.*

This reluctance was part of Buddha's belief that people are easily caught up in intellectual puzzles, and attracted to ideas that will not ultimately help them. Because he saw himself as a therapist rather than a philosopher, Buddha energetically discouraged such speculation. He once said that speaking of nirvana when you are not enlightened is like speaking of food when you are starving: it cannot help you, and may actually do you harm.

⑥ At its most basic level, the state of nirvana – enlightenment – is a transformation. It involves the complete absence of unsatisfactoriness, craving and desire. It may occur in life, and if it does the person experiencing it will continue to have a bodily existence, as the Buddha did.

⑥ Nirvana may also come at the moment of death, in which case the enlightened person will pass out of existence.

⑥ Siddhartha Gautama is called 'the Buddha' because of his teaching of these doctrines, but anyone who has achieved nirvana is a Buddha – an enlightened person.

The Teachings (Dharma) of the Buddha

Setting in Motion the Wheel of Truth: The first sermon

The first sermon the Buddha preached was in the Deer Park in Sarnath. His audience was the five bhikkus, who had not become enlightened. The sermon was called the *Dhammacakkappavattana-sutta* – 'Setting in Motion the Wheel of Truth'. Its contents were electrifying: the doctrines known as the Four Noble Truths, which form the basis of Buddhism.

In his sermon, the Buddha concentrated on the problem of desire, emphasizing that desiring what we do not have causes us suffering. The speculative philosophy of Hinduism at the time, embodied in the Upanishads, had suggested that our desires motivate our actions. This philosophy had taught that if our desire is for material things – if we mistakenly consider that material things are reality – then we will be reborn endlessly, with no chance of release from the cycle.

The Buddha spoke of the two extremes of indulgence and self-denial. His view was that enlightenment could be reached only by resisting the pull to extremes, and by following the Middle Way. He styled himself the *Tathagata* (one who has truly arrived or has reached the Truth). He told the bhikkus of his own experiences, and they recognized his enlightened state.

The Four Noble Truths

- The Noble Truth of Suffering
- The Noble Truth of the Origin of Suffering
- The Noble Truth of the Cessation of Suffering
- The Noble Truth of the Path Leading to the Cessation of Suffering

Buddha's analysis was penetrating and it presented a great challenge to his audience. This challenge is still valid today, and eagerly taken up by contemporary Buddhists. As Prince Siddhartha, Buddha was familiar with the arts of warfare and the mechanisms of government. But once he was enlightened he recognized the limitations of these techniques of social control. The greatest battle is to conquer oneself, beside which conquering others was simple and ultimately purposeless. To conquer oneself, constant self-awareness and self- criticism are necessary. It is easy enough to reject the insights of Buddha, because the world offers many distractions and some of these are very attractive in a superficial way. Yet, as they listened, the bhikkus secretly felt relief at the clarity of Buddha's message. Throughout their long years of spiritual searching they had hoped for one who would discourse with authority on the issues of vital importance in all human lives. Their relief is akin to that felt on hearing a doctor's diagnosis after a long period of being 'not quite well.' To know is better than not knowing. So what was it that they now knew?

Pu-tai, laughing pot-bellied monk.

The Four Noble Truths: Putting an end to suffering

The Four Noble Truths presented the Buddha's enlightened insights to the bhikkus.

1. The Noble Truth of Suffering

Life is suffering. Birth and death are suffering. Everything in life, whether pleasant or unpleasant, is unsatisfactory. Being in love brings thrills, but also anguish. A comfortable armchair is agreeable to relax in, but if you were to sit in it for ten hours you would be in great pain.

2. The Noble Truth of the Origin of Suffering

The origin of suffering is located in desire, thirst or *tanha* ('craving'). Human beings yearn for more even when they are quite well provided for. What is more, their yearnings are often existential and not merely material: they yearn for existence, or a longer life, and are greedy to realize their potential. Some humans also yearn for self-destruction. All of these desires prevent people from living in the moment, living in a pure manner and not desiring anything. Desire keeps people attached to the cycle of birth, death and rebirth.

3. The Noble Truth of the Cessation of Suffering

Craving and desire must vanish entirely if people are to be free from suffering and unsatisfactoriness.

4. The Noble Truth of the Path Leading to the Cessation of Suffering

This path is known as the Eightfold Path. It is also known as the Middle Path or Middle Way, because it advocates moderation.

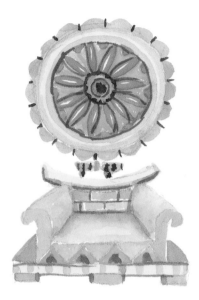

The first three truths articulate an analysis of the human condition, a diagnosis of the difficulties and pains present in life, and a prescription for curing these problems. This accords well with the view of the Buddha as a therapist or a psychologist rather than a priest. But was his diagnosis right? How could people stop craving, thirst and desire? The Eightfold Path aims to help them.

The Noble Eightfold Path: The path to transformation

The Fourth Noble Truth of the Path Leading to the Cessation of Suffering presents the Buddha's prescription for spiritual awakening. The most interesting thing about this prescription is its extreme practicality. The Buddha realized that his insights alone would not free people from dukkha, or suffering. They needed a program for structuring their lives.

This Fourth Noble Truth is known as the Eightfold Path because it offers eight ways to be free of suffering and the sense of unsatisfactoriness:

- right view
- right understanding
- right speech
- right action
- right vocation
- right application
- right recollectedness
- right contemplation

Dharmachakra-mudra: symbol of 'Wheel of the Law.'

Right view and right understanding

The first two precepts of the Noble Eightfold Path are mental requirements. If the person seeking enlightenment has attained them, this means that he or she has acquired a basic comprehension of the problem and its solution.

Right speech, right action, right vocation and right application

These constitute the 'active' part of the Path. Those who are intent on becoming enlightened must avoid all injury to living creatures, any kind of false or harmful speech, and any form of immoral or wrongful behavior.

The choice of a vocation is also crucial; any method of earning a living that brings harm to other creatures must be shunned. Defining occupations that involve harming animals or people is a complex matter. It would not be possible to be a slaughterer of animals, for example, or to have the job of preparing furs or leather for human wear. If you were a cook, the preparation of animal products could be said to cause harm, even though someone else had killed and dismembered the animal earlier. In modern terms, professions such as the law, insurance, and medicine would be problematic, because although there is the possibility that you could help people, these professions also have negative consequences (testing that harms animals, defending people who are guilty, and so on). A teacher could cause harm by intellectually or emotionally damaging students, even though teaching is a venerable profession.

Occupations that harm oneself include prostitution and thieving, but also those jobs that could involve compromising one's integrity for the sake of the business. Right application focuses attention not only on acting and working appropriately, but also on pursuing a virtuous lifestyle in a suitable way.

Right recollectedness and right contemplation

The final section of the Eightfold Path refers to the need to control thought and have a steady and consistent mental state while seeking enlightenment. Being

mindful involves retreating from thoughts that focus on the world of sense perceptions and the trivia of everyday life.

If this control is lacking, meditation, the chief spiritual exercise of Buddhism, would be impossible. Right contemplation is directly related to meditation, in that it refers to forcing the wandering mind to concentrate on one subject. A reflective attitude, which involves careful consideration of all thoughts and actions, will result from mindfulness and contemplation.

Meditation

The contemplative stage is the culmination of the Eightfold Path. This explains why, in the Buddhist view of the path to transformation, meditation is the final means to achieving nirvana.

Buddha taught *vipassana* ('insight') meditation, which is an analytical method based on mindfulness, observation, and total awareness of reality. The meditator may be totally aware of the body, the emotions, the mind and the subject of contemplation while meditating.

It is important to regard the Noble Eightfold Path as a unity rather than a sequence of steps, even though the eight elements do seem to be divided into three distinct stages.

The first two elements in the Path, right view and right understanding, involve some knowledge of basic Buddhist doctrines. Without this knowledge it would be impossible to take the actions set down in the third, fourth, fifth and sixth elements: speech, acting, selecting a vocation and applying oneself appropriately. These three things are the 'moral conduct' section of the Path. The final section of the Path, the contemplative elements, can occur only as a result of all of the other elements. But all eight elements must continue to be both active and interactive throughout the process.

Ashvaghosa's poem 'Nanda the Fair,' which explains the basics of meditation for lay people, states:

> *Whatever a man thinks about continually, to that his mind becomes inclined by force of habit. Abandoning what is unwholesome, you therefore ought to ponder what is wholesome; for that will bring you advantages in this world and help you win the highest goal [nirvana].*

Control of one's mental processes is central to the achievement of enlightenment, because in the Buddha's view humans become what they intend. The Buddha emphasised the value of recollection. This is a form of thought which enables us to be aware of our thought processes over time. Without recollection, we really know nothing; we are unaware of what is happening within ourselves.

The Spread of Buddhism

Recording Buddha's teachings

At the Council of Rajagaha after the death of the Buddha, the earliest Buddhist scriptures, commonly known as the Pali Canon, were standardized. Pali is the common spoken form of Sanskrit. The early Buddhist sangha was a community that used the oral tradition for its doctrines, rather than one that relied on written texts. The monks collectively remembered Buddha's teachings, and these were divided into three categories, known as the *Tripitaka* ('Three Baskets'). The teachings were remembered and transmitted orally until approximately 100 BC, when people began to write them down.

A religion or a philosophy?

The early Buddhist community reverenced the memory of Buddha. Yet for centuries no statues were made of him, as early Buddhism was essentially atheistic. Buddha was not a god, and therefore it was inappropriate to treat him as such. Stupas, the burial places of arhats (spiritually advanced persons), were intended to inspire Buddhists in their quest for enlightenment, and not to be 'places of worship.' This essential atheism in the early phase of Buddhism is the reason many regard Buddhism as a philosophy rather than a religion.

The Tripitaka

The Buddha's teachings were divided into three categories:

- ⊚ the *Sutra Pitaka*, which collated the sermons (*sutras*) of the Buddha
- ⊚ the *Vinaya Pitaka*, which collated the regulations governing the sangha
- ⊚ the *Abidharma Pitaka*, which collated the techniques for interpreting appropriate to the Buddha's teachings.

A second Buddhist Council was held a century after Rajagaha at Vaisali, to settle disagreements over the strictness of religious observance. Rules to lessen this strictness were rejected overwhelmingly.

At a third, non-official Council less than fifty years later, the first splinter groups appeared. The numerically smaller party, the Sthaviras, who were staunch defenders of the conservative position, prevailed.

Jainism

Despite these doctrinal disputes, Buddhism continued to grow, with Hinduism, the traditional religion of India, experiencing an eclipse. Another minority religion was Jainism (from jina, 'conqueror'), a radically ascetic sect. It was founded by **Vardamana Mahavira** ('great hero'), a contemporary of the Buddha. Like Buddha, Mahavira was of the *kshatriya* (warrior) class, and had married and had one child. He too left on a spiritual quest, but the Jain solution, radical asceticism, was much more drastic than Buddha's Middle Way. Consequently, Jainism never won great numbers of converts, and remained a small group on the Indian religious scene.

A 'world religion'

Buddhism began to expand and transform into a 'world religion' during the reign of Emperor **Ashoka**. He was the grandson of the great **Chandragupta**, who had driven the last garrisons of Alexander the Great from India. Ashoka ascended the throne in 270 BC and ruled an empire that consisted of most of northern and central India. It is said that he converted to Buddhism when he realized what suffering he had caused as a victorious military commander.

Ashoka sent missionaries to preach Buddhism locally in Sri Lanka and south India, and to countries as far abroad as Macedonia, Egypt and Syria, and he erected pillars with Buddhist inscriptions on them. These pillars are the earliest Buddhist texts. He attempted to improve the welfare of the people, using humanitarian policies and social reforms. He signed his edicts Piyadasi, 'the humane.'

Ashoka is often called 'the Second Founder of Buddhism,' and his life established a template for the Buddhist lay person. He convened the Third Buddhist Council in 247 BC at Pataliputra. By this time it was clear that there were doctrinal divisions developing within the community.

The Questions of King Milinda

The text *The Questions of King Milinda* is a record of a conversation between a Buddhist missionary, Nagasena, and King Milinda. He was the ruler of a Bactrian Greek kingdom, and was probably called 'Menander' in Greek. He, and five hundred of his courtiers, listened to Nagasena's preaching. The king was a thoughtful and scholarly man, and asked Nagasena many a difficult question. However, he was satisfied with the answers that Buddhism provided. The text says that he saw the value in the Buddha's religion. He gained confidence in the Triple Jewel, lost his spikiness and obstinacy, gained faith in the qualities of Nagasena, and became trustworthy and free from conceit and arrogance.

Kuan-Yin, the Chinese 'Goddess of Mercy.'

The Theravada and Mahayana traditions

Around 100 BC, Buddhism divided into the *Theravada* ('tradition of the elders') tradition and the *Mahayana* tradition. The Theravada group retained only the early Buddhist scriptures, and continued to believe that Buddha was merely a human being. They reverenced the *arhat* as their spiritual ideal. This group is called *Hinayana* ('lesser vehicle') by the Mahayana Buddhists. This term is generally regarded as pejorative because it implies that in Theravada Buddhism the capacity for salvation is less than in Mahayana.

In contrast, the emerging Mahayana ('greater vehicle') Buddhists welcomed new teachings and new scriptures, in the Sanskrit language at first but later also in the vernacular languages of converted countries such as China, Tibet and Japan. Mythological stories were told to explain why the new doctrines were acceptable.

In the case of the *Prajnaparamita* ('perfection of wisdom') Sutras, it was claimed that Buddha wished to teach these doctrines but found no receptive humans. He taught them to netherworld dragons, from whom the great Buddhist teacher **Nagarjuna** later learned them. Nagarjuna was then able to teach the doctrines to the Buddhist community.

Mahayana Buddhists regarded the Theravadins as fundamentalists, overly attached to the details of the human life of Siddhartha Gautama. Mahayana groups came to believe in the saving powers of beings called bodhisattvas, those who were on the point of achieving enlightenment but held off to aid the spiritually less advanced. Chief of these was **Avalokiteshvara**, the bodhisattva of infinite compassion, who in Chinese Buddhism becomes the 'goddess of mercy,' Kuan-yin.

Doctrines on the existence of other buddhas became common – for example, the buddha **Amitabha** ('unlimited light'), who reigns over the Pure Land of the West. In the forms of Buddhism where he is prominent, devotees need only recite his name in order to enjoy a blissful afterlife in the Pure Land. Another important buddha is **Mahavairocana** ('great shining out'), whose body is identical with the cosmos, and who is worshiped as the sun buddha. Then there is **Maitreya**, a messianic bodhisattva who will be the next human buddha.

These figures are often worshiped in Mahayana Buddhism. This is a continuation of the Hindu tradition of bhakti – loving devotion to a personal deity. In Mahayana, the individual does not struggle toward enlightenment unaided, but is assisted by the compassion of the bodhisattvas and buddhas.

Sri Lanka: The Theravada tradition

Ashoka sent his son Mahinda and his daughter Sanghamitta as missionaries to Sri Lanka. To recommend themselves to the Sri Lankans, they brought a cutting from the Bodhi tree and one of the Buddha's teeth. This precious relic was interred in the great stupa at Kandy, which is still a place of Buddhist pilgrimage today. The type of Buddhism which took root in Sri Lanka was Theravada, and it retains its special 'early' Buddhist character to the present era. It honors the monastic life and advocates achieving nirvana by following the Noble Eightfold Path. The only scriptures Sri Lankan Buddhists (and other Theravadan communities such as those in Thailand) accept are those collated at the First Council of Rajagaha.

For Sri Lankan Buddhists, Buddha is a man, to be reverenced and studied as one who has overcome the obstacles of human life in order to achieve enlightenment. Buddha is also seen as not being unique: there were enlightened beings before him, and there will be enlightened beings after him.

The ancient nature of Sri Lankan Buddhism was recognized in the Buddhist world. When Buddhaghosa was seeking the oldest versions of certain Buddhist texts in the fifth century AD, it was to Sri Lanka that he went.

Tibet: The Vajrayana tradition

One of the forms of Buddhism that developed in India was influenced by Tantric Hinduism. This tradition used ritual, sacred incantations, mandalas and sexual practices to achieve enlightenment. The Tantric practices were attributed to the Buddha in order to satisfy the requirements of authenticity.

This form of Buddhism traveled to Tibet, Nepal and Mongolia, where it came to be known as *Vajrayana* ('diamond vehicle'). Srong Tsan Gam Po, the king in Lhasa, the Tibetan capital, had two Buddhist wives. In 630 AD he requested that missionaries come to Tibet from India. But the missionaries were not successful;

Tibetan Buddhism stresses the opposites of maleness and femaleness among the gods and goddesses, in human life and in the cosmos itself. Sexual acts are a significant part of religious practice.

It was widely believed that sexual intercourse could be a rapid path to enlightenment. This is the tradition of the Short Path to Enlightenment,which is for those with the requisite spiritual courage. There are doctrines particular to the Buddhism of Tibet, such as the Kalachakra (time and space) teaching. This states that the whole universe moves in a cycle and the experience of time is only the functioning of the vital currents in the body, which parallel those of the universe.

the Tibetans rejected Buddhism in favor of their animistic native religion, *Bon* (pronounced 'pay-en'). However, approximately a century later a wandering preacher, **Shantarakshita**, who taught Tantric doctrine, arrived in Tibet and had immediate success in winning converts. Elements of the Bon tradition were incorporated into Buddhism: **Tara**, the mother goddess of Tibet, was widely worshiped among the Buddhists. Both the Buddhist wives of King Srong Tsan Gam Po were identified with her.

The monastic tradition was also embraced. Monasteries were built and two separate orders, the *Nyingmapa* ('Red Hats') and the *Gelugpa* ('Yellow Hats'), who reformed the earlier Red Hat doctrines, developed. Both groups were part of the Vajrayana tradition. The Red Hats ate meat, and believed that the body can assist the spiritual quest, and that sex can contribute to enlightenment.

The succession of abbots in Red Hat monasteries was by lineal descent, as the monks had sons. The reforms of the Yellow Hats involved a rejection of sex as a possible path to enlightenment, and the introduction of vegetarianism. Both groups wear red robes, the yellow hats and sashes distinguishing the Gelugpa monks. The priests of the Bon tradition were known as the Black Hats.

This type of Buddhism spread to neighboring Nepal, and was adopted later in Mongolia. It has become more popular in the West as a result of the Dalai Lama's frequent preaching tours in Western countries.

The Gelugpa order developed the doctrine of the lama ('supreme being'), who is a living Buddha. As the Gelugpa rejected sexual acts and did not have sons, they believed that the head lama of the monastic order would be reborn after death. The Dalai Lama, resident as an exile in India since 1959, is the living leader of the Gelugpa order, and the fourteenth in the line of Dalai Lamas.

The Three Jewels: the Buddha, the dharma and the sangha, the three most important aspects of Buddhism.

43

China: Ch'an Buddhism

Buddhism had reached China by the first century AD, but was not immediately successful. China was a proud and ancient civilization, with the native religious traditions of Confucianism and *Taoism*. **Confucius** had inculcated in the Chinese people a love of tradition, and a fervent nationalistic pride in all things Chinese. China's was a conservative culture.

There was a more successful Buddhist mission nearly a thousand years after Buddha's death, when a strong-minded Indian monk called **Bodhidharma** made the long journey to China hoping to win converts to Buddhism. Bodhidharma's variety of Buddhism was called 'Dhyana,' meaning 'meditation.' He concentrated on teaching people to achieve enlightenment by meditating. The Chinese were still reluctant, however, and in disgust Bodhidharma spent several years staring at a wall. However, he eventually found adventurous souls who yearned for enlightenment, and he began to appreciate the beauties of Chinese culture. Ch'an Buddhism (known in Japan as Zen – both words mean 'meditation') was born.

There were modifications to Buddhist doctrines – for example, the Chinese believed prosperity and family life were desirable, and could not comprehend asceticism – and new sutras were composed to make Buddhism acceptable to Chinese culture. Ch'an Buddhism emphasized the importance of what people did rather than what they believed.

From Taoism, Ch'an Buddhism acquired its love of the natural world. Ch'an believes that insights are not won by examining the world or by gathering information, but, rather, that insight is found in spontaneous experience. Ch'an also developed techniques to bring home to its followers the futility of intellectual pursuits. One of these was the *kung-an*, a kind of riddle where a Ch'an master asks a question, and the disciple must give a spontaneous response. There are no right or wrong answers.

In one story, a Chinese abbot wished to found a second monastery, and he needed a monk to govern it. Pointing to a drinking vessel, he asked one senior monk to tell him

One anecdote tells of Bodhidharma's meeting with the Chinese Emperor, who believed that Buddhism was about the accumulation of merit through doing good deeds. He explained what he had been doing to accumulate merit, but Bodhidharma interrupted him: 'No merit whatever!'

The Emperor's view of Buddhism was shaken, and he asked, 'What, then, is the sacred doctrine's first principle?'

The reply was, 'It's just empty. There's nothing sacred.'

The Emperor became indignant: 'Who are you, then, to instruct us?'

Bodhidharma was unruffled: 'I don't know.'

This utterance reflects Mahayana Buddhism's doctrine of sunya, the void. One famous sutra asserts that:

> *Form is not different from emptiness; emptiness is not different from form.*
> *Form is precisely emptiness; emptiness is precisely form.*

This teaching is not intended to cause Buddhists philosophical difficulties, it is intended to assist them in going beyond logic, in order to aid the process of enlightenment.

what it was without giving its name. The monk said,'You could not call it a piece of wood.' But the monastery cook kicked over the vessel and walked away. The cook was selected to run the new monastery.

The cook's reaction was appropriate: he had no concern for things, and so he kicked the object to show his disregard for it. He demonstrated that he was a man of action, not intellectual speculation. This is admired in the anti-intellectual schools of Buddhism.

Japan: Zen Buddhism

Buddhism reached Japan in the mid-sixth century AD. By the ninth century, several sects of Buddhism were present in Japan, including the Tantric Shingon and the Tendai, who focused on the *Lotus Sutra* (Buddhist scripture which contains the doctrine that all forms of existence, animate and inanimate, are filled with Buddha-nature). The introduction of Zen ideas to Japan is traditionally attributed to **Eisai**, who in the twelfth century AD imported the Rinzai school from China; however, Zen had been generally known since 700 AD. Zen is the Japanese for Ch'an, 'meditation'.

All Buddhist schools advocate meditation. The defining characteristic of Zen is naturalness. The path to enlightenment is believed to be direct. The basics of Zen are teaching, practice and enlightenment. However, these are all rather elusive. Teaching may include the study of the sutras, yet it is also possible to reject all of the sutras. The view on the 'teaching' aspect of Zen is that there are no Zen teachers. When novices enter a monastery they are assigned to a *roshi*, a 'master'. But the role of the roshi is not to teach, but rather to leave the novice to work out his or her own answers. There are two Japanese schools of Zen: Rinzai uses *koans* (equivalent of the Chinese kung-an) to stimulate novices, but *Soto* does not.

Practice is the most tangible aspect of Zen. Despite the claim that Zen has no ritual, there is a practical side to it. Ritual may not be compulsory, but most believe that reaching enlightenment is more difficult if the believer does not engage in vigorous meditation.

Zen is a true continuation of Buddha's teachings, with its focus on monasticism and meditation, but it is new too. The concept of nirvana (enlightenment), which had originally been permanent, gave way to the Japanese concept of satori (a temporary flash of awakening).

The main form of Zen meditation is called zazen, 'sitting meditation' (see page 55). Meditation is directed toward the achievement of *satori*.

*Golden Pavilion
(Kinkakuji), Kyoto, Japan.*

Satori is not permanent, as nirvana is; it is a momentary flash of truth and beauty, of knowing in the most fundamental way. This clear vision indicates a release from the illusions of this world. Although the vision may seem sudden, years of meditation and concentration on koans may be necessary before it is achieved. Often the satori experience follows an experience of intense disillusionment, when it is believed that the breakthrough will never come.

The Westernization of Buddhism

Until the eighteenth century, the prevailing Western attitude to Buddhists was that they were missionaries' potential converts to Christianity. Then the Enlightenment brought with it an interest in the world's religions as examples of how different peoples developed solutions to perennial human dilemmas. In the nineteenth century the texts of Buddhism were translated into European languages by scholars, and knowledge of Buddhism grew gradually. Movements such as *Theosophy*, a philosophy that combined Eastern and Western elements, assisted in this process.

Theosophy

The Theosophical Society was founded in New York in 1875 by Madame Helena Blavatsky and Colonel Henry Steel Olcott. Theosophy is a philosophy that combined elements of Spiritualism, the Western esoteric tradition, and religious teachings from India, where Madame Blavatsky and Colonel Olcott lived for some time. The foundation of Theosophy in America in 1875 marked the beginnings of Buddhism in that country also. Madame Blavatsky often claimed that the idea of Theosophy was not her own, but had been suggested by Tibetan Buddhist masters with whom she had studied. In 1880 Madame Blavatsky and Colonel Olcott recited the Three Jewels and the Five Precepts for lay people in Sri Lanka, and formally became Buddhists. The Colonel devoted the rest of his life to the spread of Buddhism in the West, and in Sri Lanka Olcott Day is still celebrated, as a festival of gratitude for the revival of Buddhism.

During the nineteenth century Buddhism became known as a philosophy to several distinguished Western philosophers, including Arthur Schopenhauer. But in terms of the popular spread of Buddhism, a single book had the greatest effect. One of the most popular nineteenth century best-sellers was Sir Edwin Arnold's *The Light of Asia*, which was an elaborate epic poem retelling the life of the Buddha. In some respects it was inaccurate, in that it confused certain aspects of Hinduism and Buddhism, but it did much to establish the Buddha as a 'heroic soul,' and Buddhism as a valid religion, among educated Westerners.

In the twentieth century, Buddhist organizations began sending missionaries to Western countries. In addition to this, many Asians migrated to the West, and multicultural, multiple-faith societies were gradually created. Early twentieth-century Western Buddhists were primarily attracted to the Theravadan tradition, largely because its atheistic doctrine was perceived as being compatible with the Western scientific world-view. For similar reasons, Zen became popular.

Although Western Buddhists do become monks and nuns, Buddhism in the West is generally a lay movement, and people attend Meditation Centres or Buddhist community groups rather than monasteries or temples. There has recently been an upsurge in Western interest in Tibetan Buddhism.

Finding Enlightenment

The Buddhist approach to transformation

To understand Buddhist meditation, the difficult doctrine of *pratitya-samutpada* ('dependent origination') must be examined. Dependent origination is the doctrine which demonstrates that no 'reality' actually is real. It does this by demonstrating that nothing exists of itself, but things only exist in dependence with other things. Buddha believed that the physical world was maya, 'illusion.' He also asserted that the human self was not real. Three key Buddhists terms, anatta ('no self'), anicca ('transitoriness or impermanence'), and dukkha ('suffering'), are the foundation of the Buddhist understanding of existence.

Buddha stated that the elements making up a person come together at birth and disperse at death, so there is no real 'self' that continues into the next birth, just trace elements imbued with karma. The teacher Nagasena, in the great text *The Questions of King Milinda*, uses an analogy to illuminate this difficult doctrine: the flame of the torches of the night's first watch is not the same as that of the second watch, but the second flame will be lit from the first, and the third will be lit from the second. So there is a connection between each life, even if there is no real self that continues through rebirth.

The meaning of this discourse is that the whole of human existence is a process of becoming; it is one thing becoming another. A person is a collection of impermanent psychological processes and illusory physical conditions. There is no permanent ego, which is the reason that it is one of the chief psychological processes of humans to desire passionately to bring into existence a permanent ego. Yet doing so is impossible. This is one of the reasons for the frustration of human existence.

Buddha explained the doctrine of dependent origination to his disciple Ananda as follows:

Ananda, if it be asked, 'Do old age and death depend on anything?',
the reply should be, 'Old age and death depend on birth.'
Ananda, if it be asked, 'Does birth depend on anything?',
the reply should be, 'Birth depends on existence.'
Ananda, if it be asked, 'Does existence depend on anything?',
the reply should be, 'Existence depends on attachment.'
Ananda, if it be asked, 'Does attachment depend on anything?',
the reply should be, 'Attachment depends on desire.'
Ananda, if it be asked, 'Does desire depend on anything?',
the reply should be, 'Desire depends on sensation.'
Ananda, if it be asked, 'Does sensation depend on anything?',
the reply should be, 'Sensation depends on contact.'
Ananda, if it be asked, 'Does contact depend on anything?',
the reply should be 'Contact depends on the mental and physical phenomena.'
Ananda, if it be asked, 'Do the mental and physical phenomena depend on
anything?', the reply should be, 'The mental and physical
phenomena depend on consciousness.'
Ananda, if it be asked, 'Does consciousness depend on anything?', the reply
should be, 'Consciousness depends on the mental and physical phenomena.'
Thus, Ananda, on the mental and physical phenomena depends
consciousness; on consciousness depends the mental and physical phenomena;
on mental and physical phenomena depends contact; on contact depends sensation;
on sensation depends desire; on desire depends attachment; on attachment
depends existence; on existence depends birth; on birth depends old age
and death, sorrow, misery, lamentation and grief, and despair.
Thus does this entire aggregation of misery arise.

Enlightenment and meditation

The doctrine of dependent origination makes it clear that the cycle of becoming must be broken. This means that as long as people desire existence they will pass from one life to another, and these will all be false lives. Only by ceasing to desire existence will people cease being reincarnated. This helps us to understand the attractions of the Buddhist concept of enlightenment (nirvana).

To cease to be, to escape the cycle of birth, rebirth and death, is an excellent thing, representing liberation from suffering. To achieve nirvana the Noble Eightfold Path must be followed, because it encourages moderation and cools human emotional responses.

The Zen attitude to enlightenment is paradoxical. The great master Rinzai (d.867) said:

> Just be ordinary and nothing special.
> Relieve your bowels, pass water, put on your clothes and eat your food.
> When you're tired, go and lie down.
> Ignorant people may laugh at me but the wise will understand ...
> As you go from place to place, if you regard each one as
> your own home, they will all be genuine, for when circumstances come
> you must not try to change them.
> Thus your usual habits of feeling, which make karma for the Five Hells,
> will of themselves become the Great Ocean of Liberation.

This teaching builds on the Mahayana idea that, because form and emptiness are identical, at a fundamental level samsara (the wheel of rebirth) and nirvana (liberation) are identical. This can only be grasped by the spiritually advanced. But it does mean that it may be difficult to distinguish between a happy-go-lucky, worldly person and an enlightened person who does not seem very holy as he or she has gone beyond the conventional understanding of 'holiness.'

Kensho: A permanent state of enlightenment

In early Buddhism, nirvana is variously translated as 'quenched' or 'cooled,' or 'snuffed out,' as in the case of a candle. It is understood as a permanent state: having entered into nirvana, it is not possible to revert to the world of karma and samsara. Samsara is the wheel of birth, death and rebirth, the reincarnatory cycle. The concept of nirvana appears in Zen Buddhism as *kensho*, permanent enlightenment. However, it is understood that few ever reach this state.

The more common enlightened state in Zen is satori, a condition of temporary, but very profound, awakening, characterized by a sense of naturalness and immediacy. This marks a change from Buddhism's Indian origins, where there was a great distrust of the senses and the information acquired from the natural world.

Bodhisattvas – 'enlightenment beings'

As mentioned earlier, a bodhisattva is an enlightened being – 'bodhi' means 'enlightenment,' and 'sat' means 'being.' In Mahayana Buddhism, a distinction is drawn between a bodhisattva and one who, like Siddhartha Gautama the Buddha, has passed into nirvana. Mahayana Buddhist sects regard the bodhisattva as superior because they are motivated by compassion; they want to remain in the world in order to assist others on the path to enlightenment.

In Ch'an and Zen, masters and teachers are often honored by the title of bodhisattva, but the devotion that Mahayana sects give to the bodhisattvas is entirely absent. This is partly due to Zen's lack of ritual and general attitude of skepticism toward conventional religious forms. Many of these great teachers behaved in eccentric and incomprehensible ways. For example, **Ma-tsu** was reputed to walk like a bull and glare like a tiger, and was given to shouting at his students; **Chao-chou**, when asked for instruction by a monk, asked whether he had eaten his gruel and told him to wash the bowl; and **Huang-po** would not speak, and struck novices who questioned him. These eccentric behaviors were recognized as a sign that the teacher had attained the Buddha-nature.

Zen Buddhist Meditation

Meditation: Opening your eyes to your 'true nature'

The Chinese belief that human nature is fundamentally good has profoundly influenced the doctrine of the person in Ch'an and Zen. The true nature the Zen novice seeks to attain is the Buddha-nature, and this is within, not a state external to the person. It is believed that all things possess Buddha-nature. For some Zen masters, Rinzai for example, awakening involves the courage to 'let go' and have faith that one's natural and intended state of functioning is the Buddha-nature.

This influences the attitude to work in the Zen monastery. All monks do strenuous physical labor every day; the master **Po-chang** (720–814 AD) said: 'A day of no working is a day of no eating.' Physical activity assists in breaking down mental habits that impede satori. Of utmost importance is the breaking down of

Zazen: Sitting meditation

As its name would suggest, to do zazen ('sitting meditation') one sits, either in the lotus position or the half-lotus, and concentrates on one's allotted koan. The full lotus position is believed to facilitate the unification of the mind: this is important, as Zen meditation is directed to the achievement of satori.

In a monastery, zazen takes place in a large, bare meditation hall, with the floors covered by straw matting. Each person has a cushion to sit on. The correct posture is sitting straight-backed, with the hands in the lap. Monks patrol the room; if anyone loses concentration or falls asleep, they strike the errant meditator with a stick. This blow is not punitive, but merely intended to restore concentration.

Monks also take swift, short walks during their meditation time, whenever they feel their grasp of the koan is slipping.

the distinction between one's 'self' and one's 'experiences'. The realm of pure experience is reality. The self interferes with unmediated experience, and subjects it to analysis; Zen meditation assists in clearing this block. The value of meditation is expressed in a verse from Hakuni's 'The Song of Meditation':

> *Those who perform meditation for even one session*
> *Destroy innumerable accumulated sins;*
> *How should there be wrong paths for them?*
> *The paradise of Amida Buddha is not far.*

In contrast to the koan system of Rinzai, Soto focuses on the everyday tasks with which the monks engage. Virtually all humans walk during their day. Like sitting meditation, structured walking meditation takes place in a meditation hall. It is characterized by changes in pace, and is watched over by monks who mark lapses in concentration.

Focus and concentration exercise

Make a pale-colored disc of approximately twenty centimeters in diameter, or some similar object in a neutral, non-shiny color. This form of meditation may be done sitting or standing, but sitting is best. Before you look at the disc calm your body and sit comfortably. Begin to look at the disc intently, but do not stare. The disc represents the earth, and it may help you to repeat 'earth, earth' steadily as you gaze. One aspect of this exercise is to clear your mind of unnecessary thoughts, and to focus your attention. The result of this type of meditation is that even when you are away from the disc you should be able to see it in your mind, and it will assist in keeping your mind clear. Practice this form of meditational focus for as long as you can, increasing the amount of time until you can keep the mental image with you effortlessly.

Choosing a suitable focus for meditation

Novices are often puzzled by the issue of what to focus on when attempting to meditate. Certain forms of Buddhism assert that the intention of meditation is to clear the mind. Novice meditators realize how hard this is to do: an endless stream of images, words and experiences roll through the mind like a feature film. Some of these mental events are important, but much of what clutters the mind is trivia.

Accordingly, most meditation techniques have a focus, to narrow the concentration. This may be a mantra – a repetitive statement to focus the mind in meditation – a koan, or some other object such as the qualities of the Buddha.

If mediation is to take place in a lay context, such as a home, it would be better to focus on an insight from a poem. The following poem is an example:

The morning glory which blooms for an hour
Differs not at heart from the giant pine,
Which lives for a thousand years,
is both beautiful and an expression of
a profound truth.

Kinhin: Walking meditation

Another form of meditation that is popular is *kinhin*, or walking meditation. It is more popular with the Soto sect of Zen, as Soto does not emphasize the use of the koan puzzle to attain enlightenment. Soto Buddhists believe that Rinzai's emphasis on koans creates a tendency to get stuck on intellectual issues, whereas kinhin focuses attention on the rhythms of the body.

For Soto Buddhists, the focus of meditation is 'motiveless action,' a notion that is very close to the Taoist concept of wu-wei (no action). Through this, Taoists attempt to achieve wu-hsin (no mind), and the Soto Buddhists agree that meditation should just be 'sitting just to sit' or 'walking just to walk.'

Chants, Koans, Sutras, Mantras and Poetry

Words as a focus for meditation: Poetic forms

Since the beginning of the Buddhist movement, followers have expressed their insights through the literary medium of poetry. The earliest Zen poems, which borrow heavily from Taoist ideas, investigate the nature of the universe, the way to enlightenment, and the role of nature in sparking awakening. The principle of right contemplation, from the Noble Eightfold Path, plays an important role, in that Zen poetry speaks of the need for effort and concentration:

> *The perfect way is without difficulty,*
> *Save that it avoids picking and choosing.*
> *Only when you stop liking and disliking*
> *Will all be clearly understood.*
> *A split hair's difference*
> *And heaven and earth are set apart!*
> *If you want to get to the plain truth,*
> *Be not concerned with right and wrong.*
> *The conflict between right and wrong*
> *Is the sickness of the mind.*

This early Zen poem is counseling neither anarchy nor the abandonment of morality. Rather, it is drawing attention to the way in which thinking in terms of opposites makes it difficult for us to achieve a sense of non-duality.

Square, triangle, circle – fundamental forms of the universe.

Haiku

The sudden awakening of satori is well represented in the brief poetic form of the *haiku*. In the Japanese language, a haiku consists of seventeen syllables. Natural phenomena are popular subjects for reflection, but in the context of Buddhism everyday experiences are celebrated too:

> *When cold, we gather round the hearth before the blazing fire;*
> *When hot, we sit on the bank of the mountain stream in the bamboo grove.*

Zen in Japanese culture

Zen permeates all aspects of Japanese culture, and has made a significant contribution to a number of art forms, including:

- ⑥ the Japanese art of ikebana (flower arranging), where a single blossom in a vase transcends what can be seen in a whole bouquet
- ⑥ the ritual drama of the Noh play
- ⑥ the tea ceremony, in which the everyday activity of serving tea is carried out with simplicity, and with special ritual implements, in a quiet setting.

It is a central requirement of Zen that common things be seen in a new light; seeing ordinary activities afresh may allow them to become a focus for meditation.

Mindfulness of Breathing

One very important Buddhist characteristic is 'mindfulness'. To achieve this through meditation, practice awareness of breath. Set an alarm clock to ten minutes. Sit comfortably and concentrate on the breathing sensations in your abdomen. Count your breaths in and out to ten. If your attention wanders, go back to one. Continue until the alarm goes off, then try to assess for how much of the time you were mindfully focused.

Koans and the nature of reality

In the Rinzai school of Zen there are five major categories of koans, the seemingly illogical puzzles upon which novices focus in order to achieve satori. It has been suggested that it could take a monk thirty years to complete the whole sequence of available koans.

Many scholars have objected that the intense concentration on obscure puzzles, such as Hakuin's (1685–1768 AD) famous 'What is the sound of one hand clapping?,' produce a state where the novice believes he knows absolutely nothing. It has even been claimed that this state, artificially induced by koan education, would get in the way of achieving satori. But opposites are closely related in Zen, and the effort put into attempting to reach a rational answer is designed to make the student lose faith in the process. Once rationality is abandoned, the student is able to make the leap into irrationality, and, in the answer to the koan, quite often mind, body and the koan itself are wiped out of existence.

The five koan groups

- ⑥ **hosshin, 'entering the gate of Zen':** beginners' koans.
- ⑥ **kikan:** koans focusing on the 'active expression' (i.e. testing the skill) of the state of 'entering the gate of Zen.'
- ⑥ **gonzen:** expressions of the Zen understanding of speech.
- ⑥ **nanto:** koans that are difficult to penetrate.
- ⑥ **goi:** koans related to the philosophy of the Avatamsaka Sutra.
  (The name of this sutra is usually translated as the 'garland' or 'flower ornament,' and it is the inspiration behind Hua-yen Buddhism in China and Kegon Buddhism in Japan. The central doctrine of the Avatamsaka Sutra is the interdependence of all things.)

There are several acceptable ways of answering a koan to the roshi's satisfaction. These include replying with another question, performing a charade, and responding with the koan itself. The seeming irrelevance of many of the recorded responses to koans reminds the Western person of the absolute resistance to rationality in Zen. For example, in the first hosshin stage, the seeker is encouraged to make a fool of himself or herself. It is clear that this is to lessen attachment to oneself, but often it is hard for Western devotees to accept. Sometimes it is necessary to ponder earlier answers to koans; Chao-chou answered 'no' to the question 'Does a dog have Buddha nature?' Students are asked why that was his answer. Roshis have no patience with philosophical answers; they want to be shown, and students offer stones and sticks, hand gestures and face-pulling as possible solutions.

Another vital aspect of the koan education system is that you have to find out the answer for yourself. There is a Chinese proverb: 'What comes in through the

gate is not family treasure,' and Zen Buddhists believe this means that what is told to you by another is not your own knowledge. So the student must fight his or her way through doubts and fears, through false solutions and relief – which is often mistaken for satori – until a genuine realization is reached.

For the lay practitioner of Zen this intensive training is not necessary, and koans are most often used as a minor adjunct to meditation. However, the lesson they teach – that it is necessary to give up on traditional methods of reasoning and take a leap into the unknown – is an important one for all Buddhists. For it is habit and familiar patterns that keep people attached to this life, and prevent them from approaching the freedom of enlightenment. Western people are especially attached to the life of the mind, and their 'philosophical' orientation is generally far from that of Buddhism.

Chanting and mantras

Chanting is a strongly recommended activity in Buddhist monasteries, and the most common chant used among Zen monks is the 'Four Great Vows of a Bodhisattva.' This states:

All beings, without number, I vow to liberate;
endless blind passion I vow to uproot;
dharma gates beyond measure I vow to penetrate;
the Great Way of Buddha I vow to attain.

This is a lofty sentiment, and it is of spiritual benefit to reflect mindfully on what it means. The use of mantras was traditional in Hinduism, and has been carried over into Buddhism. The repetitive nature of the mantra helps to focus the mind during meditation. Chanting functions in much the same way, quieting the mind and shifting the chanter's state of consciousness until quite a different type of mental clarity is achieved. The mantra is of especial importance in Pure Land Buddhism, where it is believed that repetition of the phrase 'namu Amida butsu' ('I take refuge in the name of Amida Buddha') results in salvation in the Pure Land of the West. Mantras are used less frequently in the Zen tradition.

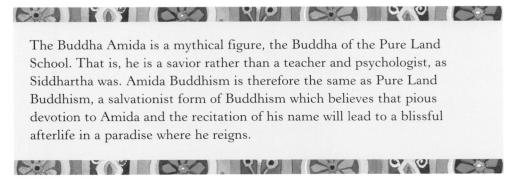

The Buddha Amida is a mythical figure, the Buddha of the Pure Land School. That is, he is a savior rather than a teacher and psychologist, as Siddhartha was. Amida Buddhism is therefore the same as Pure Land Buddhism, a salvationist form of Buddhism which believes that pious devotion to Amida and the recitation of his name will lead to a blissful afterlife in a paradise where he reigns.

The wisdom of the sutras

Zen Buddhism explicitly rejects formal dependence on the sutras, the Buddhist scriptures. Nevertheless, they are read and loved by many Buddhists the world over, and some Zen practitioners know them intimately. What is important in Zen is that it is understood that however helpful such texts may be, they cannot lead directly to an enlightened state.

Different sutras expound different Buddhist doctrines. For example, the Sukhavati-vyuha Sutra, the 'sutra on the vision of the land of happiness,' describes the Pure Land paradise of Amida Buddhism as follows:

It exists infinitely far away on the western edge of the universe; it is surrounded on all sides by beautiful terraces, on which grow magical trees whose branches and twigs are made of precious stones. When a gentle breeze blows, the twigs and branches lightly rub together and produce marvelous music. There are pools and lakes there, lined with precious stones and sprinkled with lovely lotuses. Blossoms shower down, and the whole of this world is pervaded with light and perfume. The gloriously plumed birds sing the praises of the Buddha and of his law, his dharma. The pious who dwell in this celestial paradise are reminded at every turn of the glories of the faith, and offer flowers to the Buddha as a token of their reverence and esteem.

The purpose of such a text is to remind the Buddhist devotee how much more desirable is the spiritual reality than is the world in which humans struggle to live. It is not necessary to believe in the Pure Land literally, although it is clear that at the level of popular piety many people do. Other sutras, such as the Prajnaparamita-hrdaya Sutra ('Heart Sutra'), discourse on more complex theological subjects. Here the central doctrine is that 'form is emptiness and emptiness is form,' which has been discussed earlier. This important phrase from the Heart Sutra may be used as a meditational aid, as it is suitably brief and expresses a crucial doctrine. With meditative recitation, the most important aspect is to remain sharply aware of what you are saying. If you lose track of the meaning, cease reciting for five minutes, then begin again in a mindful state.

It is important to realize that, in Buddhist thought, emptiness is not equivalent to non-being. It has often been contended that to claim that all is empty eventually undermines religion, ethics, and even existence. But this conclusion depends on viewing emptiness as an essentially negative thing. Fa-tsang, a Chinese master of the Hua-yen School, wrote a text called the *Hua-yeni-ch'eng chiao i fen-ch'i chang* at the end of the seventh century AD. In it he argued that emptiness was interdependence. In an analogy designed to demonstrate that everything is not merely part of the whole, but that each individual is in fact identical with the whole ('all is one'), Fa-tsang speaks of a rafter in a building:

Any individual – symbolized here by a rafter – possesses six characteristics, or marks, through the possession of which the relationships of identity and interdependence pertain. Thus any individual, such as the rafter in the building, simultaneously possesses the characteristics of universality, particularity, identity, difference, integration and disintegration. In other words, then, the rafter will be a particular object with its own clear-cut appearance and function but at the same time will be universal, that is, it will be the building, or totality, and so on. The 'one' referred to in the sentence concerning universality is the building, or, by extension, any totality.

This is the realization that what we had thought of as our individual being is in fact contingent upon a myriad of other beings, both animate and inanimate. This text inspires a feeling of respect and gratitude; in Hua-yen Buddhism, the world is nothing but the co-operation and support of the beings that constitute it.

Famous Buddhists

Nagarjuna

Nagarjuna was born in the second century AD, into a Brahmin Hindu family in south India. He converted to Mahayana Buddhism as a young man, and became an influential teacher. His most famous work is the *Mulamadhyaamakakarika* ('basic verses on the Middle Way'). His main teachings were on emptiness and the sunya ('the void'), and he insisted that there were two kinds of truth, the ordinary and the higher. He was also interested in clarifying the relationship between Buddhist practice and theory.

The void was a central concept in Mahayana Buddhism, also sometimes called the 'emptiness teaching.' The intention of this teaching was to show that all supposed realities were entirely arbitrary.

Shinran

Shinran (1173–1262 AD) founded the Jodoshinshu or True Pure Land school. At the age of nine he became a monk in the Tendai sect, but when he was nearly thirty he had a vision that led him to Honen, the founder of Pure Land in Japan. His sect was more radical than Honen's, for he dissolved monastic vows, married and had several children. His teaching was that of the need for a passionate devotional piety whereby the believer clings to the compassionate Buddha Amida.

Incorporating Buddhism in Your Daily Life

Gaining the benefits of Buddhism

Alan Watts, a distinguished scholar of Zen with a particular interest in communicating Zen principles to Westerners, once wrote:

True Zen is just eating when you are hungry, and sleeping when you are tired.

What he meant is that the Buddha wanted people to be freed from their cravings – for love, for material possessions, and so on. He wanted people to be able to live in the moment, free from anxiety. As Watts suggests, this is so often not the case with us. How often do we feel hungry, but wait, because 'It's not yet lunch-time'?

It is actually true that it is better for our physical and mental health to eat when we are hungry and sleep when we are tired. It is a characteristic of modern Western people that we live profoundly unnatural lives. Our sleep cycles are not matched with the pattern of the sun; instead, we often work or play long into the night. We have designated times and places for eating and sleeping. Many of us deny ourselves food and sleep as part of a personal game of discipline. These things encourage us to turn food and sleep into fetishes, and do not allow us to recognize them for what they really are.

*So, if you are interested in Buddhism and have read a little
or attended lectures, or have friends who are practicing Buddhists,
how do you go about gaining the benefits of Buddhism
in your daily life?*

Even without a spiritual master you can find and read poems and mantras to repeat or focus on when you need to calm down or when you are facing difficulties. These techniques will not remove the human facts of pain and mortality, but they can help you to cultivate a serene acceptance of the reality of human life.

Let go of anxieties about trivial things, and focus on those things that are of lasting importance in human life. At some point all of us will have to look back on our lives and ask whether they have been worthwhile, whether we have concentrated on the important things. Modern life contains so many distractions that it is often difficult to remain focused on those things that are going to last the distance.

Buddhism stresses the need for us to rid ourselves of cravings and desires that can only be destructive. This involves understanding and accepting yourself as you are.

The Buddhist lifestyle: Suggestions for living harmoniously

Many Buddhists take the principles of the Ten Precepts seriously, and seek to avoid alcohol and all intoxicants. They become vegetarians, and also refuse to wear leather or use any products that may have involved harm to animals during the manufacturing process. Allowing a 'Buddhist' flavor to penetrate your life does not necessarily involve all of these lifestyle changes. But there are many practical things you can do to allow the characteristic Buddhist sense of calm to enter your life more fully.

Your living environment

In your living environment, avoid clutter and aim for simple, clear and soothing pieces of furniture, colors and personal possessions. Your environment may often cause distress because it intrudes into your mind. In contrast, think of the beauty and simplicity of Japanese flower arrangements, and the bare cleanness of Japanese houses. It is not necessary to have a home exactly like this, but the principles do apply.

It is also important to have the natural environment close to you. If you do not have a garden, grow flowers and herbs in window boxes and pots. If even this is impossible, put up posters of, say, cherry trees in bloom or of great Californian redwoods.

Practicing even a few Zen rituals will help with lowering stress, and may make you more outgoing and more willing to connect with others by forming new social relationships and communities. Many people withdraw from such activities because they feel they are too busy. Meditating and simplifying your life will give you a greater sense of liberty with your time.

In time, Zen may make productive contributions to all areas of your life, and greatly improve your happiness and feelings of self-esteem.

Meditating at home

If you intend to meditate at home, an orderly, uncluttered room will be more conducive to focusing your mind. Music may help to set your mood. Certain types of music are always calming and helpful; Mozart's compositions are probably the best known in this category.

Your main intention, when making these Zen Buddhist modifications to your life, should be the achievement of the state of 'sitting quietly, doing nothing.' Just as the body needs sleep, so does the mind need quiet times for recharging and refocusing. The modern lifestyle is more stressful than that of the past, and we are generally less connected to our community than previous generations were. Aspects of everyday life can contribute to the effectiveness of meditation. For example, it is suggested by some Buddhist teachers that when you realize that you are awake, sharpen focus immediately and concentrate deeply on awareness of being awake. This can be an important technique in personal relations also; mindfulness teaches that if you begin to feel anger or distress you should focus closely on the particular emotion manifesting itself and prevent it from directing your responses and actions.

Living in the moment: Integrating mind and body

The West has traditionally made a sharp distinction between the mind and the body, the spiritual and the physical, the everyday and the sacred. Zen Buddhism seeks to break down these distinctions, insisting that a focus on opposites fragments reality. See the poem quoted on page 58:

> A *split hair's difference*
> And *heaven and earth are set apart!*

The Zen aim is to keep heaven and earth, body and soul, and mind and body together. This will integrate us and counter the feeling of fragmentedness that many report experiencing in the modern world.

If you can abandon your worries about the future, and all recriminations and regrets about the past, you can begin living in the moment. Attempting to do so, even at a very basic level, will bring a Buddhist quality into your life. Add to this meditation or the reading of Buddhist scriptures, and the underlying philosophy of the necessity for 'letting go' will become clearer.

People who have achieved the state of 'letting go' are not callous, nor is it true that they don't care about the past, the future, or others. In fact, through living in the moment, they will be more able to give of themselves selflessly, and may make wiser decisions about their own lives.

No guru, no method, no teacher: Finding the truth for ourselves

In traditional Japanese Zen, the relationship between the master and the student is of vital importance. Asian cultures place great emphasis on the need for the student to admit ignorance and the master to administer discipline, as this will lead the student into a position of knowledge.

However, when a religion or philosophy crosses cultures, different emphases develop. Some Western Buddhists may be eager to experience a relationship with a roshi, but many others take a different approach. Many Western people are interested in, and even deeply engaged in, Buddhism without being 'Buddhists.' For these people, introducing meditation into their daily lives, cultivating a sense of the beauty and reality of the natural world, and diminishing their ego-centeredness are ideals that are not necessarily 'religious.' They constitute a philosophy well equipped to deal with the stresses of modern urban life. In this case, there is no need for a guru or roshi, or for withdrawing from the world into a monastery.

The essence of Buddhism is simply the desire to live in the moment, appreciating the interconnectedness of people and nature. Meditation, reading, or one's ordinary daily tasks may be 'devotional activities' in that they lead to the achievement of this goal.

Reading More about Buddhism

Conze, E., *Buddhism*, Munshiram Manoharlal Publishers, India, 1999.

Conze, E., *Buddhist Scriptures*, Penguin, Harmondsworth, 1964.

Conze, E., *Buddhist Texts Throughout the Ages*, One World Publications, Oxford, 1997.

Harvey, P., *An Introduction to Buddhism*, Cambridge University Press, Cambridge, 1990.

Herrigal, E., *Zen in the Art of Archery*, Arkana, London, 1989.

Kapleau, P., *Awakening Zen*, Prentice Hall, London, 1997.

Ling, T., *The Buddha*, Gower Publishing Ltd, Hampshire, 1973.

Lowenstein, T., *The Vision of the Buddha*, Macmillan/Duncan Baird, London, 1996.

Rahula, W., *What the Buddha Taught*, Gordon Fraser, London, 1980.

Skilton, A., *A Concise History of Buddhism*, Windhorse, Birmingham, 1994.

Suzuki, D. T., *Awakening of Zen*, Shambala Publishing, Boston, 2000.

Suzuki, D. T., *Essays in Zen Buddhism*, Grove Press/Atlantic Monthly Press, New York, 1961.

Watts, A., *The Way of Zen*, Vintage, New York, 1989.

Glossary

Abidharma Pitaka   the 'basket' of scriptures concerned with the interpretation of the Buddha's sermons

ahimsa   the fundamental Buddhist principle of doing no harm

Amida Buddhism   Buddhism according to the Buddha Amida

anatta   'no soul' – a negation of the existence of the Brahman, or world-soul

anicca   Buddhist term, meaning transitoriness or impermanence

arhat   spiritually advanced person

asceticism   the practice of severe self-discipline, severe abstinence often in solitude

atman in Hinduism, an individual soul which is reunited with the world-soul (Brahman) when enlightenment is reached

Avatamsaka Sutra the Buddha's 'flower ornament' sermon

bhikku Hindu forest monk

bhikkuni nun

Bodhi knowledge or enlightenment

Bodhi tree knowledge tree, under which Siddhartha sat awaiting enlightenment

bodhisattva one who is going to become a buddha; an 'enlightenment being'

Bon animistic native religion of the Tibetans

Book of the Great Decease text describing Buddha's death

Brahman in Hinduism, the world-soul

Brahmin Hindu priestly class

Buddha the 'enlightened one'

buddha, a an enlightened being

Buddhacarita 'Acts of the Buddha,' a biography of the Buddha

caste Indian hereditary class with members usually equal, united in religion and following the same trade; four main groups: Brahmins, Kshatriya, vaishya and Sudra

Dalai Lama chief lama and ruler of Tibet

Dhammacakkappavattana-sutta 'Setting in Motion the Wheel of Truth,' first sermon of the Buddha

Dhammapada important early Buddhist scripture

dharma teachings, law of the Buddha

dukkha Sanskrit for 'suffering,' or 'unsatisfactoriness'

ego the self

Eightfold Path the Fourth Noble Truth preached by the Buddha, the Noble Truth of the Path Leading to the Cessation of Suffering

Gelugpa Yellow Hats

guru spiritual teacher in Hinduism

haiku form of Japanese poetry, a poem with seventeen syllables

Hinayana 'lesser vehicle,' derogatory term for Theravada Buddhism

Hinduism dominant religion of India; its main characteristics are the worship of many gods, a caste system, and a belief in reincarnation

Hua-yen Buddhism Buddhist group with the belief that the world is nothing but the co-operation and support of the beings that constitute it

Jainism a minority religion in India, radically ascetic

jina 'conqueror,' enlightened person in Jainism

karma 'action,' the actions that tie humans to the cycle of birth and rebirth

kensho in Zen Buddhism, a permanent state of enlightenment

kinhin meditation walking meditation

koan puzzle posed to students in Zen Buddhism, intended to break rational thought

Kshatriya the warrior class in Hinduism

kung-an kind of riddle where a Ch'an master asks a question, and a disciple must give a spontaneous response; see koan

lama 'supreme being,' chief priest or monk of Mahayana Buddhism

Laws of Manu traditional laws governing Hindu life

Lotus Sutra Buddhist scripture which contains the doctrine that all forms of existence, animate and inanimate, are filled with Buddha-nature.

Mahavastu 'Great Event,' a biography of the Buddha

Mahayana Buddhism 'greater vehicle': form of Buddhism found in China, Japan, Korea and Vietnam that welcomed new teachings and new scriptures

Middle Way the path of moderation advocated by the Buddha

moksha 'liberation,' spiritual goal in Hinduism

Mulamadhyaamakakarika 'basic verses on the Middle Way,' text by Nagarjuna

nirvana 'cooled' or 'quenched'; in Buddhism means enlightenment

Noble Eightfold Path a set of principles leading to cessation of suffering

Nyingmapa Red Hats, a subsection of Vajrayana Buddhism

Pali Canon see Tripitaka

Parinirvana trance state preceding entry into nirvana

Prajnaparamita Sutras sermons on the 'perfection of wisdom'

Prajnaparamita-hrdaya Sutra 'Heart Sutra'

Pratitya-samutpada concept of 'dependent origination'

Pure Land Buddhism salvationist form of Buddhism; believes that pious devotion to the Buddha Amida and the recitation of his name will lead to a blissful afterlife

reincarnation the belief that when the body dies the soul is reborn in another body

Rinzai a Japanese school of Zen, uses koans

rishi master or teacher in Hinduism

roshi master or teacher in Zen Buddhism

sangha the Buddhist monastic order

Sanskrit the language of ancient India

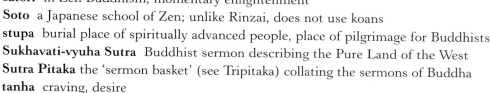

satori in Zen Buddhism, momentary enlightenment

Soto a Japanese school of Zen; unlike Rinzai, does not use koans

stupa burial place of spiritually advanced people, place of pilgrimage for Buddhists

Sukhavati-vyuha Sutra Buddhist sermon describing the Pure Land of the West

Sutra Pitaka the 'sermon basket' (see Tripitaka) collating the sermons of Buddha

tanha craving, desire

Taoism philosophical and religious system of ancient China

Tathagata 'one who has achieved Truth,' a title of the Buddha

Ten Precepts the Buddha's precepts that regulate the ethical conduct of Buddhist monks and nuns, as well as lay Buddhists

theosophy a philosophy combining Eastern and Western elements

Theravada Buddhism the 'tradition of the elders,' a form of Buddhism found in Sri Lanka, Laos and Thailand; believes that Buddha was merely a human being

Therigatha 'songs of the elders,' early Buddhist poems composed by monks and nuns

Three Jewels the Buddha, the dharma and the sangha, the three most important aspects of Buddhism

Tripitaka the earliest Buddhist scriptures, known as the Pali Canon; meaning the 'Three Baskets,' it focuses on three main areas; for example, see Vinaya Pitaka

Upanishads Hindu texts dating from 800–500 BC which contain speculative ideas

Vajrayana Buddhism 'diamond vehicle': form of Buddhism found in Tibet, Nepal and Mongolia and influenced by Tantric Hinduism

Vinaya Pitaka the 'sangha basket' from the Tripitaka, giving rules for monastic life

Vipassana 'insight' meditation, an analytic method based on mindfulness, observation, and total awareness of reality

yoga Sanskrit word meaning union of mind, body, and spirit

Zen Japanese for Ch'an, 'meditation'

List of Names

Alara Kalama spiritual teacher of the Buddha

Amitabha the buddha of 'unlimited light,' who reigns over the Pure Land of the West

Ananda Buddha's relative and most beloved disciple

Ashoka Buddhist emperor in the third century BC, who signed himself 'Piyadasi' ('the humane'); often called 'the Second Founder of Buddhism'

Ashvaghosha poet in the first century AD, author of the Buddhacarita ('Acts of the Buddha')

Avalokiteshvara bodhisattva of infinite compassion; in Chinese Buddhism, the 'goddess of mercy,' Kuan-yin

Bodhidharma Indian monk, introduced the 'Dhyana' (meditation) form of Buddhism, which became Ch'an Buddhism

Buddha 'Enlightened One,' name given to Siddhartha Gautama

Chao-chou Zen master

Chandragupta drove the last garrisons of Alexander the Great from India

Confucius Chinese philosopher and teacher of ethics

Devadatta cousin of the Buddha, cause of a split in the sangha and attacks on the life of Buddha

Dhammapada a famous Buddhist scripture

Eisai bringer of Zen ideas to Japan

Fa-tsang a Chinese master of the Hua-yen School

Hakuin seventeenth century Zen master, inventor of the koan system

Huang-po Zen master

Kshantivardin 'preacher of patience,' a forest ascetic; a former life of the Buddha

Ma-tsu Zen master

Mahaprajapati aunt and foster-mother of the Buddha, first ordained Buddhist nun

Mahasattva a prince who sacrificed himself to feed a tigress who was dying of hunger; a former life of the Buddha

Mahavairocana ('great shining out') a buddha whose body is identical with the cosmos, and who is worshiped as the sun buddha

Mahinda son of Ashoka

Maitreya a messianic bodhisattva who will be the next human buddha

Mara Hindu demon-god of desire and worldly attachment

Maya mother of the Buddha

Moggallana one of Buddha's chief disciples from early on

Nagarjuna distinguished Buddhist interpreter, second century AD

Nandabala alternative name for Sujata

Po-chang Zen master, 720–814 AD

Rahula 'impediment,' son of the Buddha

Sanghamitta daughter of Ashoka

Sariputta one of Buddha's chief disciples from early on

Shakyamuni 'sage of the Shakyas,' a title of the Buddha

Shantarakshita wandering Buddhist preacher who taught Tantric doctrine in Tibet

Shuddodhana father of Siddhartha Gautama

Siddhartha Gautama known as the Buddha ('Enlightened One')

Sujata compassionate young village girl who gave Siddhartha food after his long struggle with fasting and asceticism

Tara the mother goddess of Tibet, widely worshiped among Buddhists

Uddaka Ramaputta spiritual teacher of the Buddha

Upali monk left in charge of Buddhist community, together with Ananda, after the death of the Buddha

Vardamana Mahavira founder of Jainism

Yasodhara wife of the Buddha

First published in Canada in 2001 by
Raincoast Books
9050 Shaughnessy Street
Vancouver, B.C. V6P 6E5
(604) 323 7100
www.raincoast.com

Commissioned by Deborah Nixon
Production Manager: Sally Stokes
Text: Carole M. Cusack
Designer: Avril Makula
Editor: Avril Janks
Illustrator: Penny Lovelock
Project Co-ordinator: Kate Merrifield

Canadian Cataloguing-in-Publication-Data
Cusack, Carole M.
The essence of Buddhism
ISBN 1-55192-385-8
1. Zen Buddhism.   2. Buddhism--Doctrines.   I. Title.
BQ9265.4.C87 2001   294.3'927   C00-911511-0

Set in Revival and ITC Novarese on QuarkXPress
Printed in Singapore by Tien Wah Press (Pte) Ltd